# MOS_ DRY FEET

Exodus 13:17–15:21 for children

### Written by Joan E. Curren
### Illustrated by Ron Wheeler

**Arch® Books**
Copyright © 1998 Concordia Publishing House
3558 S. Jefferson Avenue, St. Louis, MO 63118-3968
1-800-325-3040 • www.cph.org

Manufactured in Colombia

The Pharaoh's men were gaining ground.
Their sleek chariots were rolling
So fast behind the horses strong,
Eyes wild and nostrils foaming.

God's people saw the chariots,
The horsemen, and the army.
The shields and spears shone in the sun.
It started such an outcry.

"They're gaining on us!" was the shout.
We stumbled as we hurried
Through sand that slowed our footsore steps.
God's followers were worried.

We moved so slow, uncounted throng,
With sheep and goats and cattle.
And now the Red Sea in our path
May force us to do battle.

God's people were so terrified.
They wept and moaned and shouted.
"We cannot stand against their might.
On horses they are mounted.

"They'll capture us and drag us back.
With whips and chains they'll beat us.
We'll work from dawn past setting sun.
Oh, God, will they defeat us?"

"Oh, God," I prayed, "You brought us here
Away from our oppression.
You've been our strength; our faith's in You.
We claim Your love's attention.

"You've led us with Your cloud by day.
Night's darkness You have broken
By fiery pillar guiding us.
Your love for us You've spoken."

The Lord then spoke to me and said
That we should never worry.
He would fight the fight for us
And in that way gain glory.

The Lord said, "Stop your questions now
And tell folks to quit moaning.
So forward, march! Pick up those feet
And get the people going!"

God moved the cloud from front to back
Between our camp and Pharaoh's.
The blackest night surrounded them,
But on our side bright light glowed.

I stretched my hand toward the sea.
A miracle was coming.
The sea was split by God's east wind.
The path was dry by morning.

Between the high and watery walls,
We crossed the Red Sea bottom.
When Pharaoh's army tried the same,
The walls collapsed and drowned them.

We stood astounded on the shore,
Then thrilled to God's great mercy.
We shouted, prayed, and sang our songs
Of praise to God in glory.

Then Miriam, with timbrel bright,
Led ladies in their dancing.
They spun and twirled and leaped and whirled.
The picture was entrancing.

So pray to God; He'll hear your prayers
And help when you're in need.
Remember what He did for us
And follow where He leads.

Dear Parents:

God has worked many miracles for you and your child, just as He did for the Israelites. One of these miracles is the gift of faith. God sent His Son, Jesus, into this world to live, die, and rise again to win us forgiveness and eternal life. God gives us the gift of His Holy Spirit to work faith in our hearts so we believe the Good News of our salvation. Just as the Israelites celebrated the parting of the Red Sea, we can celebrate the miracle of faith every day.

The next time your child takes a bath, encourage him or her to attempt to "part the water" in the tub. After several attempts, emphasize that, for humans, this is impossible. Only God has the power to work such a miracle. Remind your child of the miracle of faith, then pray together, thanking God for all His good gifts.

The Editor